Further Praise for *This Geography of Thorns*

J. Todd Hawkins's *This Geography of Thorns* is an autumnal journey through the vivid and moving lives and soundscapes that bore the great Blues singers through their triumphs, sorrows, and often too-brief time on earth. Throughout, Hawkins excavates the hard memories of the music: "What demons / fathered such blues?" . . . "In the corner shadow, / we watch ghosts choke whiskey / from old throats." Echoing Cain's fatal words to Abel, the dark lines of the opening poem recall Frank Stanford's South: "Some still say / you must go out into the fields / & whisper a death to the bees." Keen images underlie a strong sense of Place in Hawkins's verse, pulling the reader in with ". . . sweet, smoky creosote seeping / from rail ties," and "kudzu blooms, / honeysuckle, water hyacinth." In poems like "Shooting at Tornadoes" and "The Red Gift," we witness the Blues' wider ground, where some have slept "in the gauzy fields / of rain" and where lovers play out their sensual lives "in the sodium glow / of parking lot lamps / . . . / in the wet pines" where "the minty smoke" from a young woman's cigarettes leaves the tongue of her lover. Included in this territory are its folklore and magic—a coal oil bottle holding "Killing & kissing light"—where rage is expressed against nature's terror, as "The river & the air know no border," and "the cottonmouth / . . . / eats "a rain of dust / from our feet." Fecund landscapes abound in "the flesh-eating wildflower / that sprouts from acid bogs," the troubled soil of the Delta, the ground of some of its oldest and often obscure haunts, where "under a curtain of birdsong, / the wind sifting boil dust over the deep black soil," "the sharp metal flavor of sleeplessness." Though poignantly autumnal, *This Geography of Thorns* is not wholly sorrowful, "Because the blues / . . . / are not simply sadnesses. / They are lights onto paths." With as strong a sense of Place as any Southern writer, Hawkins gives us a memorable collection, one with an eloquent sense of joy and sorrow, both luminous and haunting.

> — Jeffrey Alfier,
> Founder and co-editor of Blue Horse Press
> and *San Pedro River Review*

Be prepared for a ride on the soul train as you open J. Todd Hawkins's new and powerful collection of poems. Even if you have never visited the Mississippi Delta, you will know so much about it from reading *This Geography of Thorns* that you can carry on an informed conversation with residents from Clarksdale, Beauregard, Bentonia, Morehead, Walls and Lyons, Vicksburg and Memphis, just some of the places where Hawkins's poems are set or from which he derives his inspiration. The poems are filled with Delta quotidian life, flora and fauna, fortunes and misfortunes including flesh-eating wild flowers, fire ants, and spiderlings, Johnson grass, coreopsis, gandy dancing, jukes, as well as tornado sirens and the sorrows of the Lorraine. The poems are a panegyric to the bluesmen and women whose ghosts still haunt the Delta—Muddy Waters, Son House, Bukka White (whose first name was Booker but misunderstood by his producer), Blind Lemon Jefferson, and of course B. B. King. Their voices, music, and legendary, even epic, accomplishments and tribulations form the foundation for Hawkins's wide and impressive variety of poetic forms and patterns. Like the music that provided the historical trail that Hawkins follows, his poems are often so memorably grounded in lyrical wonder and beauty—in one poem we hear about the "waltz of angels" and in another we hear "the invisible swirl of words spinning from stars." Beyond question, Hawkins has written a major collection of poems that must be included in any discussion of Delta poetry today and way beyond.

— Philip C. Kolin,
Distinguished Professor of English at the Univ. of Southern Mississippi
Emeritus Editor of *The Southern Quarterly*
Author of *Emmett Till in Different States: Poems*

I relish the times I'm reading a book of poetry and the lines convince my ears I'm sitting in an old joint listening to a band cutting things to bits. It doesn't happen often, but when it does I'm hooked, forever. That's definitely the case with J. Todd Hawkins's new collection, *This Geography of Thorns*. There's blues in these fine poems, for sure, but a whole lot more joy, with language that sways and strikes like snake tattoos on a muscled arm. Poem by poem, Hawkins lays his melodies down like a master bluesman, and I feel blessed to have sat a while listening to him play.

— Jack B. Bedell,
Poet Laureate, State of Louisiana, 2017-2019
Author of *No Brother, This Storm*

Also by J. Todd Hawkins

Ten Counties Away

What Happens When We Leave
winner of the 2018 William D. Barney Memorial Chapbook Contest

This Geography of Thorns

Blues Poetry
from the Mississippi Delta & Beyond

J. Todd Hawkins

The Poetry Society of Texas

This publication is the winner of the Poetry Society of Texas's 2019 Catherine Case Lubbe Manuscript Prize competition. The judge was Adam Tavel. In accordance with contest rules, this book has been published by the Poetry Society of Texas.

This competition is an annual contest with a deadline of August 1. Complete rules and guidelines are available from
poetrysocietyoftexas.org
7059 Spring Valley Road
Dallas, TX 75254

FIRST EDITION

Publisher: Poetry Society of Texas
Editor: Susan Maxwell Campbell
Cover Art: Wesley Tingey (www.wesleytingey.com) on Unsplash
Cover Design: J. Todd Hawkins

ISBN 9798646198328

Available from Amazon.com and other bookstores

for Shannon,
my travel companion through it all

FOREWORD

Haunted, meditative, and lyrical, *This Geography of Thorns* takes readers on an engrossing, Dantesque sojourn through the American south in search of that most authentic of American artforms: the blues. To call this book a mere homage to the blues, however, would be a disservice to its heart, its sophistication, and its astute avoidance of cliché. Polyphonic and brimming with myths, these poems express the inherent complexities not only among the blues, but also among its most famous and tragic practitioners such as the legendary Robert Johnson. Sacred and profane, aching and hopeful, sparse and decadent, the blues has, much like the land that made it, always been rife with contradictions. These poems lay bare that evocative emotional force while simultaneously acknowledging the inscrutable mystery at its core. Like midnight smoke in a juke joint, it can be sensed but not held.

This alone would make *This Geography of Thorns* an impressive collection, but these poems offer far more. First and foremost, they recognize the grim historical legacies of both slavery and sharecropping, honoring the tenacity of African-American communities to make art in the face of oppression, injustice, and terror. And like the blues, they transgress the unspoken boundaries between high art and low, so readers are just as likely to observe how "mist thickens on magnolia leaves" or where "a river carries old names" as they are to witness discarded bottles in a gutter, or the depravity of seedy motels, or a man bathing with a water hose. Startlingly imagistic, page after page stuns with rich descriptions of southern landscapes, reminding us that poetry, music, and our very survival are inescapably rooted in the survival of our ecology. Finally, this work is a testament to craft. From their charmed titles to their taut lines, these poems sing a language all their own—alliterative, muscular, and lush.

Reader, you hold in your hands a book of "phantoms, / wind, & bees." Prepare to roam the Delta, where "the hot moon rose / fractured as / a million moons / among spatterdocks / in the lake." Where "they indulge strangers / only with birdshot." Where "they baptized their children with sky." It is not one tale, but a snaking country road steeped with tales, and "it begins here. / Among these rooms, / bowls of ghosts, of names."

Adam Tavel
Judge, 2019 Catherine Case Lubbe Manuscript Contest
September 2019

TABLE OF CONTENTS

A RIVER OF FACES

Beekeeping in Mississippi   3
Whippoorwill's-Boots   5
Jelly's Travels   6
She Stomps for Snakes   8
Ding. Dong. Bell.   10
The Death of Leroy Lee   12
Loved by All   14
The World Lit by the Tail Lights of an '82 Buick   18
Wild Women Don't Have the Blues   19
Gandy Dancing   22
The Egg Carton Is a Row of Witches' Hats   24
The Truth Year   25
Hurry Up Moonlight   27
The Red Gift   29
Tornado Sirens   30
Shooting at Tornadoes   31
Getting the Black Cat Bone   33
String Figures   34
The Piñata Maker's Ghost   36

SOUNDS IN THE GROWING DARKNESS

Blues for Murder Only   39
Matchbox Blues   41
The Bentonia Sound   43
Big Road Blues   45
Bug Juice Blues, Revisited   46
Burr Clover Blues   47
Gutbucket Blues   49
Grits Ain't Groceries   51
Monday Fever Blues   54
When You Let Him in the Room   55

Where the Southern Cross the Dog   57
Slow Drag   59
The Future of Courage   60
Me & The Devil & Ike Zimmerman   61
Grave Decorations   63

THE JOURNEY ITSELF HOME
Flood Gate   67
The Balcony of the Lorraine Motel   68
Baptist Town   70
Abbay & Leatherman Plantation   72
Mother Rachel's Palm & Card   74
Arriving at the Riverside Hotel by Night 76
Po' Monkey's Lounge   78
Hooks Brothers   80
We Let Them Think They're Alone   82
A Flame of Bees   83
Down in the Bottom   84
Three Forks Store   85
The Storm at Commerce Landing   87
Spoonful of Diamonds   88
In Gratitude   90
Sunset Limited   91
Return to Avalon   92
Low Country Road   94
Catfish Row   95

Some Personae   97
Acknowledgements   100
About the Author   102

A River of Faces

Well, I am a rambling kid, I've been rambling all of my days.
Yes, I am a rambling kid, I've been rambling all of my days.
Well, you know my baby she want me to stop rambling,
So she says she'll change her ways.
> — Muddy Waters, "Ramblin' Kid Blues"

BEEKEEPING IN MISSISSIPPI

Some still say
you must go out into the fields
& whisper a death to the bees.
Or else the bees, too, will die.
For years, she braved stickers
& snakes, redbugs & spiders,
wading into oceans
of vines to harvest kudzu blooms.
She'd emerge with baskets
full of flowers. Pale & long & thin
like the fingers of a teenaged girl.
Later, she'd distill their sweetness.
Add water. Lemon juice. Pectin.
She said it tasted like crabapple.
Or maybe plum.
The jars were sunshine
among the boiling pots
& browned calendar photos on her wall.
She sold the yellow preserves
to friends & neighbors
& general store owners
on both sides of the river
from Arcola to Friar's Point.
Each jar was smudged
with handwritten words:
God Bless.

After that last winter, the jelly refused
to set up. She would reboil it
over & over, trying to recall
the balance of ingredients.
When she passed, honey dripped
from the eaves above the door.
There was no one
to go through the kettles & pans,
the piles of mason jars

[3]

& stacks of cheesecloth.
Still, a few people,
the elders in the church
where she had been married once,
waded into the kudzu
to stare at the sunlight shattering
among creeping vines
to whisper—nothing.

WHIPPOORWILL'S-BOOTS

Cameron Parish, Louisiana

when we first met
I remembered
the flesh-eating wildflower
that sprouts from acid bogs
near where I grew up

not because they must
deceive to live
or because their yellow
flowers hang
face downward
shying away
from the crane-white moon
not because the stalks
grow long, graceful, bare

I remembered them
because the leaves
& the flower
seem separate plants
upon first glance
but those savvy with secrets
know they're tied, connected
with shared roots
unseen underground

[5]

JELLY'S TRAVELS

Clarksdale, Mississippi, 1908
after Jelly Roll Morton

He would call them "joys"—
the mad, frenetic stomps, the rags,
the arrangements dripping
with the Spanish tinge.
He would call them joys
because they were the farthest thing
from the blues he could think of.
They were the contrablues,
the antiblues, the unblues.

                peaches in the road
                a good week past rotten
                when he arrives

He came through here. Winning enough
at pool to buy a bag of salt & some Coca-Cola.
He'd mix the two & sell the potion
as a tonic to consumptives. A dollar a bottle.
At night, he sought the rough honky tonks
& jukes. Any place with a piano.
Places where the women would do the ham dance—
a can-can performed without undergarments.
The dancers kicking at a side of pork
hanging from the rafters.
& he would know what to play for them.
Always. He would play them joys.

                dawn through cracked glass
                flies in the washbasin
                floating

When that boy died after his doctoring,
he decided it was time to move on.
Eventually, he made it to Helena
& then Memphis, & while Gayoso Street
wasn't Basin Street, the brothels paid well
& the women were cleaner
& everywhere there was a piano.
He always said it was city life that suited him best.
                    the song ends
                    his cigarette
                    has burned down

SHE STOMPS FOR SNAKES
for Willa Mae Buckner

This house is full of stinging snakes, crawling in my bed—
I can't rest at night from them crawling all under my head.

Hmmmmmm, where is my stinging snake now?
I believe to my soul, that my stinging snake's trying to put me down.
   — Memphis Minnie, "Stinging Snake Blues"

I have never seen tattoos like this before.
Not even on the boxers
in the Eastside gyms back home.
Look. He can make the snake sway, dance,
&—he warns—strike.
In fact, the whole fleshy menagerie
trembles slowly, uneasily.
These are the sort of tattoos
people would pay to see.
But still they are nothing, he says,
to what she had.
I pass the bottle back to him.

He first saw her at the Midnight Ramble.
After the last snake act,
they kicked out the kids
& sold more tickets to the men
who stuck around,
& they all stuck around.
He saw her silhouetted
by the yellow-orange kerosene light.
The curtain rose.
Standing there naked,
motionless, her body sharp as a fang.
The local law allowed it,
as long as she didn't move.
After three minutes, the curtain fell.

He flips a lit cigarette across every finger.
Whispers how she ran away from home
at twelve to join a tent show.
Learned to swallow swords
& strip tease. Sing raunchy songs
& charm snakes.
The Snake Lady
who made poetry out of cussing.
They came for miles
to hear her sing.

He pulls hard
from the fifth of Four Roses.
Stops looking at me.
Outside, the air folds
under the weight of the river.
The band & the endless churn of crickets,
synching, out of synch.

Before the end of it all,
she even played Carnegie Hall.
By then, she lived in a small house
with pythons. Sixteen-foot-long pythons
that slept with her in her bed.
A dozen baby pythons
that slept in her pillow,
coiled around her snubnose .38
& she would call them
by stomping on the floorboards.
She would stomp,
& snakes would pour
from dark corners.
Seep from shadows.
From everywhere.
They would come to her.

His ash spills over his fingers.

Ding. Dong. Bell.

I walked the path to the well
the queen of cattails
a dandelion duchess
I felt the siren cool
& I leaned & I fell myself
in

above: a fieldstone carousel
rimmed in ranchmen—
all of them
had overstepped
not just Johnny
Flynn

the ground has memory
its holes beg
to be filled by ropes
by the wait for the water
by the arms of Tommy
Stout

but nothing can reach
as far as the sky
below, past clocks
& rabbits & doubt
nothing falls as fast as my
out

THE DEATH OF LEROY LEE

Lyon, Mississippi

Hear the banty crow
at the backdoor.
He is a splash of feathers
in the half-light.

When a rooster crows
in the house,
Mama used to say,
means a stranger is coming.

We kick rusted lids,
green glass bottle ends.
We peel back rotten wood
& peer in the windows.

In the corner shadow,
we watch ghosts choke whiskey
from old throats. We see phantom skin
wrap the pistol.

We hear
in echoes
yells of triumph,
revulsion.

Outside a house party here in 1928,
Son House's uncle was shot
in the ankle
by a stray bullet.

Son, he stared down
at that mess of a foot,
heard his uncle
crying out.

Son pulled his .38,
sneaked in through a broken window,
& shot the gunman. Shot him dead.
Right there. Shot him dead.

Someone brought Son a can of booze,
moved the women out, lit his cigarette.
Someone cranked the Victrola
while they talked.

When the sheriff got the news,
he sent the wagon.
                    But, then again,
perhaps it wasn't here at all.

Nearby, we hear children play
ring games, sing before school.
"Old folks, old folks, better go to bed,
afore you get the Devil in the young folks' head."

Morning barely seeps
from the bayou deadwater.
Nine-foot-long burlap sacks
lie stacked on the sagging porch.

On the walls, dawn's gray glow
climbs. & the rain
falls in the dust,
softly, softly,

Fire ants scatter—
each falling
raindrop
a flood.

LOVED BY ALL

New Park Cemetery, Memphis, Tennessee

We drove through
a rough part of town
to get here. Now, we cannot tell
if we are still in it.
We talk

about how cemeteries belie
the world
around them. Obscure
the border
between living & dead.

Blur differences
among the many kinds of death.
We pass stuffed animals
nailed to a phone pole—
the child's mourners.

Faux leather couch,
cracked, stained. Outside,
mist thickens on magnolia leaves.
The woman at the desk
making arrangements, crying.

& me? Ma'am, all I want
is to vanish, unimportantly,
dissolve into pocket lint
& pen caps & hide
in pleather canyons of this couch.

All I want is to know
where to find the grave
of Bukka White,
cousin of BB King,
Prince of the Blues.

The assistant to the office manager
gestures me outside.
She is out the door, in her car,
& down the road
toward the burial plat called Devotion.

I am supposed to try to follow.
We stop after a time. Ten steps
from the road. It is a small marker,
level with the turf, so as not to be in the way
of the mowers.

Indeed, it is mostly covered
in mown grass. I reach down
& wave away a summer's worth.
Perhaps not even the wind
comes here.

Booker W. White. 1909 – 1977. Loved By All.
The letters already filling with rain.
"Bukka" was the name given him
by the white producer from Vocalion,
who misunderstood his Mississippi drawl.

I think of his fingers, impossibly thick,
sliding & thumping on the neck
of his National Tri-Cone.
The whining slide of his bottle neck
whipping the frets.

I think of the time
he did in Parchman.
I think of his "Fixin' to Die Blues."
& the way Dylan played it.
I look up.

My guide is gone.
Already driven halfway
to the Garden of Peace,
just past Lower Good Shepherd.
To the grave of Rufus Thomas

or perhaps to one of the Bar-Kays
buried here
after the plane crash.
She just knew
I would want to see them next.

Her car vanishes
over the ridge.
Umbrellas flare
a flock of worried birds—
the funeral ends.

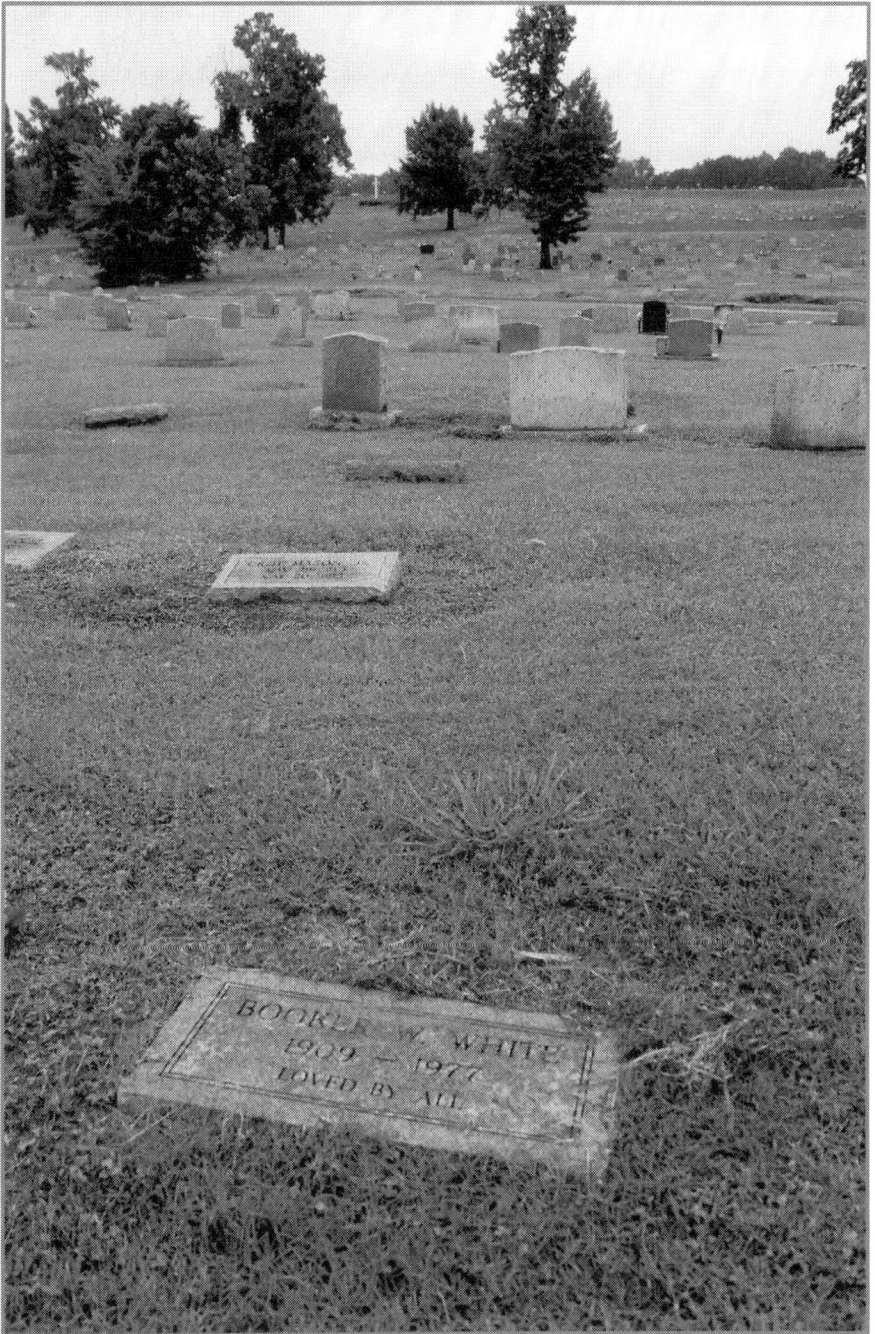

BOOKER ~~ WHITE
1909 — 1977
LOVED BY ALL

THE WORLD LIT BY THE TAIL LIGHTS OF AN '82 BUICK

behind the hotel
the kiss
hot & yellow
in the sodium glow
of parking lot lamps
& the whisper promise
to keep it hot

further
in the wet pines
the minty smoke
from her Newport
leaves his tongue

WILD WOMEN DON'T HAVE THE BLUES

New Hope MB Church Cemetery, Walls, Mississippi

What was it like,
to have joined in line
after the casket was lowered?

Or was there no one? After all,
it had been decades since she had played.
The likes of Bukka White no longer understood.

"I see Memphis Minnie," he said once.
"You know, she got fat as a butterball, that woman did,
& all she do is sit in her wheelchair & cry & cry."

He had said these things
after visiting her at Jell Nursing Home.
After her second stroke.

I've read the house where she lived
will be razed,
if it hasn't been already.

It falls in on its own weight, sagging, begging
for fire, for a room full of starlight to finish
its sad slow quaking into dirt.

Look around this place, this return
to the cotton from the city, this return
to ground from stars. Did they bury her with a gun?

When she came back from Chicago with Son Joe,
she carried a Style 1 National Tri-Cone.
No one in Jackson had ever seen a guitar like that.

Its twang cut silent
even those at the back of the room.
Through the bare-bulb haze,

[19]

its nickel-plated body shone
like a fresh razor.
That was her first reign as queen.

& today is her second.
Here, in this dominion, this wet field,
between the rail & the small highway,

its tight turns still evoking her danger.
Here, under a curtain of birdsong,
the wind sifting boll dust over the deep black soil,

the Johnson grass slapping her gravestone
in syncopation:
Memphis. Minnie. Memphis. Minnie—

while primrose
wait for night
to open.

LIZZIE "KID DOUGLAS" LAWLERS
aka
MEMPHIS MINNIE
JUNE 3, 1897
AUG 6, 1973

GANDY DANCING

A thunderous machine.
Awful, really.
I don't know its name,
perhaps because there are no songs
about it. At least not any I know.
It straddles the track,
driving spikes in ties,
crawling on its belly.
In a few minutes, I suspect
it does work
that would've taken a section crew
an hour. Or a day.
The old man I ask
tells me it is a pneumatic spike driver,
& from the looks of it,
probably one with a digital roller gauge
& fancy reciprocating spiker.
It's loud, I say. He grins.

> *up & down this road I go,*
> *skipping & dodging a .44*

Over a few quarts in paper sacks,
I come to know him.
How he called track
for a work gang decades ago.
How he would wheel a spike maul,
make it sing. How with his team
he would pull a gandy pole,
prying track into alignment
after it had been displaced
by the boundless weight
of freight cars carrying cotton,
carrying rock, carrying—
The songs, the calls came to him
in dreams, he said.

[22]

He could once go ten hours
from can-see to can't
& never repeat one.
He had never married,
but helped raise his sister's kid
for a few summers.

   Suzie, Suzie, don't you know:
   I can make your belly grow

But now, he had forgotten all the calls.
At least for me, he had.
Said he needed the tap
of the metal tools on the rails
to get the cadence right.
But it wasn't worth it.
He never wanted to hear that sound again.
His hands scarred from the creosote peel,
a life sweating into ties.
His shoulder useless from leaning
on lining bars. He looked at the spiker
as it plodded down the track.
Listened to the banging of the hammer
striking with 2,200 pounds of force
each whack. & he smiled again.

   boy I wish ol boss was blind
   so I could pull this track in line

THE EGG CARTON IS A ROW OF WITCHES' HATS

in October
black stains
on my hands
but by April
it is pastel
daisies, curling
blooming unnatural
shades from
pipe-cleaner stems
I'd cut
yours for you
when the teacher
wasn't looking
In the evenings
I practiced
playing touch
tone songs
on the phone
Mary Had a Little Lamb
3-2-1-2-3-3-3
I learned to tie my shoes
so I could tie yours
All the ways
I'd try
to impress you
breaking
dozens of eggs
just for the cups
of molded pulp
leaving shells
piled forever
in secret places,
forgotten bones
of birth

THE TRUTH YEAR

When I am young, I unscrew
the receiver of my sister's
pink rotary phone, me
a Roger Moore looking for bugs.
Inside I place a small rubber
cockroach.

During grace, she whispers
to me that she must've lost
a band-aid
in the potato salad.

At night, I slip out
the window onto the roof
when everyone is asleep
to smoke cigarettes I shoplifted,
each cloud of smoke an apology
to the neighbor's cancer.

We see on the news
her ex-boyfriend
died in a car accident.
Once, a buddy of mine
offered to take a pipe
or a bike chain to his knees.
No questions asked.

In the back of the closet,
the cat licks the infection
from the wound
she will die from.
She will hide it from us
until it is too late.

She will be the last one
to know all my secrets.

Outside, ten leagues below
the famine moon,
I follow a strand of yarn
laid miles away, there
berry blossoms grow
from a coyote's split nose.

HURRY UP MOONLIGHT

Lord, I'm almost dyin', gasping for my breath.
And a triflin' woman waiting to celebrate my death.
    — Blind Lemon Jefferson, "Hangman's Blues"

the tumblers turn
in the deadbolt downstairs
not even the alley cat
pads more softly
but still, the first chamber
stays empty—
time to think

THE RED GIFT

macadam road
the dust plumes high
behind him
the sound of the tires
when he stops
like a wild cat
choking on prey
& the light in his mouth
as he watches her smoke
curl in his headlights

TORNADO SIRENS

The sky turned deep jade.
The air swirled the hay.
I was a child again.
Being taken to the storm shelter:
Weak. Feeling the need to cry,
but knowing it was not the right place to cry.
A child blown away
by something as untouchable as wind.

I thought of not only the old ways undone,
but the new world that had been made
in what must have been only a few short minutes.

Winds scatter words,
shredded letter on the floor:
Plans.
Change.

SHOOTING AT TORNADOES

How pleasant it is
to shoulder a shotgun
toward the night
& shoot the invisible
swirl of words
spinning from stars
on thin strings.
Invasion, murder
shatter in powder.
Thoughts & *prayers*, so close
together, I crumple them both
with one shot.
I don't love you anymore,
ventilated.
Cancer is slower, so
I lead it less,
the sharp beak of its *C*
barely trailing the muzzle.

So when the storm comes
to take me, as I know
it must, I will not go
smilingly, mattresses leaning
against the walls
of a windowless room.
I will not cower
in the cold cellar
under the backyard,
staring at spiders
& old cans of
potted meats.
No, I will raise a barrel
into the air
& I will fire

over & over
until the sky bleeds
& the metal melts
& the winds wrap my body
like a kicking fly spinning in silk.

GETTING THE BLACK CAT BONE
after Zora Neale Hurston

When I first learned what you'd done,
there was the pinch in my chest.
That climbing sense of end.

& I remembered the way I felt
when I learned how Hurston
got her black cat bone.

The way she boiled the cat alive.
Melted it into fur & tallow & foam
& cursed it every time it shrieked in pain

& then passed its bones
through her mouth
until she found the right one.

STRING FIGURES

cat's whiskers
       Jacob's ladder
cup & saucer
       she showed me
witch's house
       candle thief

when it was
       my turn: moth
two coyotes
       crow's feet
carrying wood
       many stars
path to the river

werewolves
       in the back woods
she warned
       hook-handed man
Bloody Mary

tie-snake
       in the shadows
I said
       birds of the dark

if the fox's bark
       is not answered
by another's
       it wasn't the fox
who called

[34]

in the evening lawn
      the hot moon rose
fractured as
      a million moons
among spatterdocks
      in the lake

you took my hands
      & there was only
one name
      for everything

THE PIÑATA MAKER'S GHOST

darkness falls
the scent of newsprint
flowers

snow moon
inside the spaces
left for candy

the shapes of fingers
in the flour
November wind

old paste
hardens in buckets
the hungry cat's eyes

in the corner
a scrap of girl
broken too soon

SOUNDS IN THE GROWING DARKNESS

The light in this room is of a lamp. Its flame in the glass is of the dry, silent & famished delicateness of the latest lateness of the night, & of such ultimate, such holiness of silence & peace that all on earth & within extremist remembrance seems suspended upon it in perfection as upon reflective water: & I feel that if I can by utter quietness succeed in not disturbing this silence, in not so much as touching this plain of water, I can tell you anything within realm of God, whatsoever it may be, that I wish to tell you, & that what so ever it may be, you will not be able to help but understand it.
— James Agee & Walker Evans, *Let Us Now Praise Famous Men*

BLUES FOR MURDER ONLY

Crowley, Texas

You gonna keep on messin' round, honey
until you get my goat
Remember, I got a razor
& you got a great big throat
            — Pink Anderson & Simmie Dooley, "Papa's 'Bout to Get Mad"

All night they are in & out
of the mobile command center,
holding cups of coffee
or winking flashlights
past moonless creases.

Their beams only make the darkness seem darker.
The generator inside is so loud.
It shakes the pictures on our bedroom wall.
We turn out the lights. We peek through blinds
in the bay window. We are the closest neighbors
who have not been evacuated.

By "faint smell of death,"
the responding officer
would later say to the reporters,
he had meant "the smell of old blood."

It is hard to explain to a child why
there are words like SWAT,
so we do not try.
We put her antsy body back
in bed, roll her tongue up
into her mouth, tuck her questions tight

under unicorn patterned blankets.
It is probably not the right thing to do.

Because I cannot look her in the eye
as I sing softly her favorite hymns.
Songs that do not tolerate things
like tear gas or grotesque uses for ovens.
Lights swirl blue & red, grab wildly from ceilings
with long, scooping handfuls. Almost beautifully.

Unseen, seven crows fly south overhead,
black against blackness.
They are subtractors of the air.
Colder weather is coming.
We pull the pictures off the wall so we can sleep.

MATCHBOX BLUES

I'm sittin' here wondering—
will a matchbox hold my clothes.
I ain't got many matches,
but I got so far to go.
　　　— Blind Lemon Jefferson, "Matchbox Blues"

She would relish in Jack's broken crown.
& she was fierce in other ways, too.
Ways that made me smile.
I knew she would do well for herself
in a place like this.

Which isn't to say she wasn't tender,
pliable, even soft: unexpectedly.
She would always cry at the wolf's death,
no matter how many pigs or goats
or grandmothers he ate.

She would pluck the heads off dandelions
but never blow them away. Instead,
she would stroke them gently with her muddy palm.
So that not a single seed ever left her.
What child has this gift? we would wonder.

I come to this place once more. I remember
those days when everything about her was small.
Even after the taste of bubblegum cigars
& the sharp metal flavor of sleeplessness had faded.

Her hands, fingers, ears: tiny.
Her impossibly small toes threatening to disappear.
Her thin chest. Her breath.
In those days, even time itself was small.

& there was also that time
when one small box
would hold
all her things.

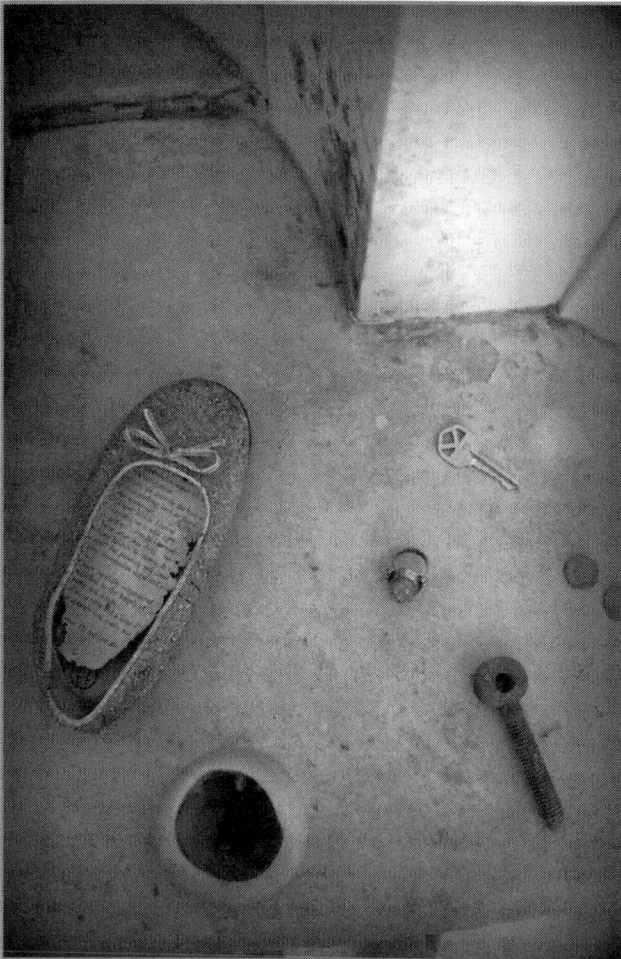

THE BENTONIA SOUND

near Bentonia, Mississippi

We stop
because it's an old-time looking store,
& she loves those,
as long as she doesn't have to use the restroom.
Or maybe we stopped
because we were thirsty
or because the kids had to pee
or maybe because we were lost
but knew we were close to the Blue Front Café.
The liner notes we were using
for a guide book told us
it was the oldest juke left in those parts,
where Skip James developed the Bentonia Sound,
the Bentonia Blues, the Bentonia School,
even though some say there's no such thing,
that it's only a breed of blues,
undeserving of its own species.
Hell, who knows why we stopped.

                    summer evening
                    drifting on the warm wind
                    spiderlings

Inside, the clerk told us how far we were.
How we should have never left the main road.
Then for no reason,
she told me she had just lost her mother.
She stared at me. Said she had just gotten the call,
how unexpected it was.
That she had not even had time yet
to talk to anyone.
That the Coke & candy would be $3.74.
& I thought—horribly—how death

should always be expected,
how it is living that should surprise us.
& when the telephone rang behind her,
I paid & left, into the coming night,
shooing moths out of my lighted path.

> late night phone call
> Mother's voice—
> "go look at the moon"

BIG ROAD BLUES

There's burned out Sterno
under the coffee tureen
in the hotel lobby. I can't stop
thinking about Tommy Johnson's
"Canned Heat Blues."
What it takes
for a man to want
to squeeze the foul jelly
through a sock,
dripping the liquid into a pot,
& drinking enough of the stuff
to catch a high.
Sock wine.
Squeeze juice.
What demons
fathered such blues? I wonder.
Then, I sip the coffee.

BUG JUICE BLUES, REVISITED

> *Love my bug juice, just as crazy about it as I can be*
> *. . . Lord, I'm afraid it's gonna poison me.*
>   — Kid Prince Moore, "Bug Juice Blues"

separating his body
& shaking himself apart
to find love

flying from place to place
to belt the lust
flashing in his red eyes

the cicada's song
rattles an empty forest
behold: the blues

BURR CLOVER BLUES

Stovall Farms, near Clarksdale

I am the vine; you are the branches. If you remain in me & I in you,
you will bear much fruit; apart from me you can do nothing. If you
do not remain in me, you are like a branch that is thrown away &
withers; such branches are picked up, thrown into the fire & burned.
   — John 15:5-6

I come from a place of horse cripplers,
detested by Cortez, & bois d'ark,
whose massive vestigial spikes
once fended off hungry mastodons.

It is a place of pale-leafed mesquite, twisted
branches studded with iron nails.
Grandparents, who had known it the longest,
called it the devil tree.

It is a land of needles, spikes, hooks, nettles.
Then, I am not such a stranger
here, really, among your catbriar, your slouching
tangles of dewberry.

I know the taste of mayhaw jelly
is sweeter because of the spines
that guard the fruit.
I know this geography of thorns.

Past the Big House, after the drive
down Burnt Cane Road,
we park in the grass. Planks lie scattered
in the weeds, dandelions, thistles.

My hand runs along the hewn cypress
sides of the old sharecropper shack
where Muddy Waters lived.
I invite the splinters into me.

At one time, these fields were filled
with burr clover. Colonel Stovall invented
a harvester for it & asked Muddy Waters
to write a song about the crop.

He wrote his song, his praise
for the thorns, his blues.

GUTBUCKET BLUES

Now mama ashes to ashes, an' it's dust to dust,
Corn liquor daddy done hushed his fuss.
— Lewis Black, "Corn Liquor Blues"

My son sees the three-string cigar box guitar
in the store window & he cannot look away.
The bright red box, the hardwood plank,
machine heads glistening in the filtered light.
Half-childtoy, half-mantool.
& then there is the washtub bass.
Bull fiddle. Gutbucket.
Like Will Shade played for the Memphis Jug Band.
Really, just a broomstick, a strip of catgut,
& a metal washtub.
You'd think anyone could manage one.

"Daddy, can you make me one?" he asks.

But my family recipes are not suited
for this sort of thing. I remember one:
        25 pounds crack corn
        6 packs yeast
        10 gallons water
        15 pounds sugar
        heat water
        stir in corn
        add sugar
        pitch mash
        sleep with the pistol
        pay the sheriff
There's more. & I remember it all.
I hold his shoulder, which is to say,
I cannot help you, Son.

Later in the hotel,
I twist open the plastic bottle of RC
& pour it into the Solo cup
with the ice & whiskey.
From the bed, a woman
whose name I'll not remember:

"Daddy, can you make me one?"

Yes. Sure. Anything you want.

GRITS AIN'T GROCERIES
Memphis, Tennessee

A hack band's "Mustang Sally" stumbles
out of Handy Park. She flows
past the overflowing toilets of Dryer's
where they deep fry burgers
in one-hundred-year-old grease.
She ambles along Beale,
past the Irish diving goats at Silky's,
past the tourist voodoo shops.
(Ride, Sally, ride.)
She goes past the overpriced,
underpoured beer at B.B. King's,
the mounted police, the frat boys
swilling syrupy hurricanes.
(All you wanna do is ride around, Sally.)
Past the street performer kids
backflipping over & over
an impossible number of times
down the gentle slope of brick.
(You been running all over the town now.)
Away from the river.
She mixes in the red shadow
of the Peabody Hotel.
(Ride, Sally, ride.)
& she turns & she stops
at A. Schwab Dry Goods Store.
The last original business on Beale.
"If you can't find it at Schwab's,
you're better off without it," they'd say.
(Think you better slow your mustang down.)
The old display windows
& the polished wood floors.
The racks of conqueroo root
& bins of rubber band guns.

(I guess I'll have to put your flat feet on the ground.)
She stops here to peer inside.
She stops to try the handle,
breathe clouds on the pane glass,
write her message with her finger.
(One of these early mornings, oh,
you gonna be wiping your weeping eyes.)
In the corner of the door frame,
a spider eats her web
as she goes.

MONDAY FEVER BLUES

the dancers' feet
on the cypress plank floor
shuffle, step, shuffle, drag
each movement
parts the smoke
scours away
boll dust
& the thin drops
of lung blood

WHEN YOU LET HIM IN THE ROOM
cento after Kitty Wells

I.
Surely there's a place to rest
a tortured mind.
Since sundown
I've been walking with these blues:
the blue of your eyes,
a well with no water.

II.
You see her there
at the bar
next to Jukebox Lane
just beyond the moon.
It was you who lied:
"She's no angel.
Her wings are not real.
Everybody's somebody's baby."
As sure as there's heaven
beyond the sun:
a woman never forgets
the little things you do.

III.
When your time comes,
I wonder what you'll do,
the waltz of the angels,
the moonlight, you.
Each Sunday afternoon
do you expect a reward from God?

IV.
As I sit here tonight,
in Heartbreak, U.S.A —
the jukebox playin',
four walls to hear me:
"It's a shame that all the blame
is on us women."

V.
Let the sunshine in.
Face it—
A honky tonk woman's
as good as a honky tonk man.

WHERE THE SOUTHERN CROSS THE DOG

intersection of the Southern R.R. &
the Yazoo Delta ("Yellow Dog") R.R.
Moorhead, Mississippi

We used to sit out in the country & see the trains go by, watch the
sparks come out of the smokestack. That was smokestack lightning.
— Howlin' Wolf

The night we held hands,
sitting on the banks of Wixon Slough,
staring at stars, trying to fill the spaces between.
Most of your time was spent
trying to explain spaces those days,
which is impossible, really,
when you think about it.

                    the creek
                    bankweed bottles
                    half in, half out

We dreamed of days when the water
would again wash over the earth. Stroke
those weedy stems, make them dance
like hair barely below the muddy ripples.
It might just be enough to soften the land,
to allow us to pull our roots & take them to Itta Bena
or farther.

The chips of flint we picked up off the ground,
the stories of Indians we let run, screaming
& yipping through our nights. Did I ever tell you
I was scared? & the train, we could feel it
long before we saw the plume of smoke
flecked with light. We could feel the ground
shake & you said it was positively

[57]

the second strongest thing you knew.
Then, you showed me some chords
you said you had made up.
I think I would have believed anything you said.

      dreams of lightning
      then remembering nothing but
      waking up

SLOW DRAG

We all know that our love can kill us.
But also, the things we touch,
the simple things we use
to make our lives, they too
can become too strong to bear.

It is said Madame Curie's papers
are still too radioactive to handle.
That even her cookbook
must be preserved
in a lead box.

In Vicksburg, postbellum genteel kept
the siege-time cannonballs embedded
in their parlor walls. Conversation pieces.
Until the powder inside
destabilized & they began to explode.

& so it is with dances
like the slow drag . . .
His arm
on her thin waist:
widow spiders.

THE FUTURE OF COURAGE

boy's open eyes
the first night
too old for lullabies

so instead, waiting in bed
for his first blues
to come wheezing

through the window screen
& bend the promise
given by dawn

ME & THE DEVIL & IKE ZIMMERMAN

Beauregard, Mississippi

Robert Johnson left
Robinsonville a decent harp player,
who could force a few licks on guitar.
He left the impatient chiding,
the berating laughs
of Son House, Willie Brown, the others.
Left the wet breasts of young lovers.
It was the winter of 1929,
& this is where he came.
He came looking for his father.
The man he found was Ike Zimmerman.
& Zimmerman taught him the blues.

This is how it happened:
They made away to the graveyard.
Plucked themselves from back porch hen chatter,
from the store front spit-&-whittle stumps.
They were closer here. Closer in.
The tomb rock thicket. When he was done,
he went back north
& people said he had sold his soul to Satan
in exchange for such a gift.

There's a river carries old names through here.
Still, after decades. A river that brings his song.
Runs the length from bridge to head.
Curls around the frets
as his raw fingers made ripples,
small splashing sounds in the murky water.

These dark cypresses recall the melody.
They sway a skeleton juke dance,
jump up out of the stony ground.
A song for no man to own.

At night, the chant of frogs
is a syncopated chorus pulsing
in & out of the trees.
Their brown bodies grow & shrink
in the pine straw.

GRAVE DECORATIONS

Little Zion M.B. Church Cemetery, Greenwood, Mississippi

> headlights through fog
> on the dashboard
> the funeral card

Maybe you wanted it a secret,
a grave by the highway.
So your spirit could catch
a Greyhound & ride.
Or maybe this, beneath the pecan,
whose leaves wither, turn the color
of bonded whisky. & then fall, skin
crumbling through veins. A death
within life. Fresh moss
may have covered your marker
had you been Basho or Issa.
But, no, not here. Not you.
Instead, a pile of beer bottles,
swept into the bowl of a hollow tree
by some caretaker. & a row of guitar picks,
bottle caps, silken flowers whose petals
frayed to strings by the sun,
the way the sun takes apart everything.

> in the churchyard
> we searched for you—
> then, the crow's shadow

How many autumns was it for you?
Not even snows to count your winters by.
Just the endless procession of offerings,
the wealth you may have wanted.
All the same, I have brought nothing.
It's embarrassing. This is supposed to be

[63]

the grave of Robert Johnson, "King of the Delta Blues."
Or maybe not.
All we have today is the decades-old memory
of the undertaker's daughter, who remembered his name.
& she remembered this tree,
far in the back of the cemetery on Money Road.

      the corn field
      the pecan tree's shade
      the space between

THE JOURNEY ITSELF HOME

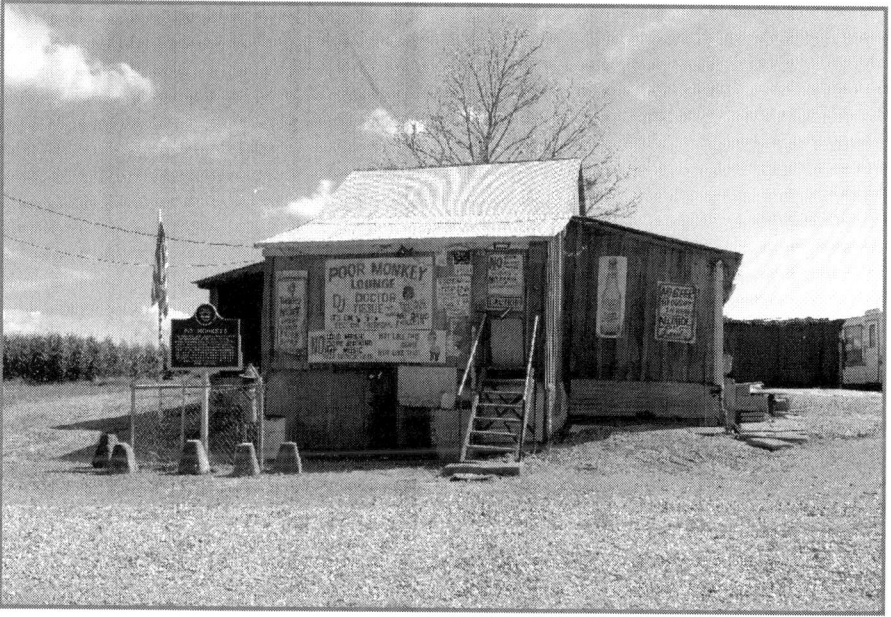

Months & days are the wayfarers of a hundred generations; the years too, going & coming, are wanderers. For those who drift life away on a boat, for those who meet age leading a horse by the mouth, each day is a journey, the journey itself home. Among ancients, too, many died on a journey. & so I too—for how many years—drawn by a cloud wisp wind, have been unable to stop thoughts of rambling.
    — Matsuo Basho, *Narrow Road to the Interior*

FLOOD GATE

New Orleans, Louisiana

from the levee,
I see the parade
of autumn
come to stop
in the black backwaters
beer cans, shrimp nets
thin swats of cypress—
the krewe of boreas

they say now
the storms are over
for the season
the high water mark
on my skin
still damp

above, the wind
swirls softly
but enough to rend
the clouds
to unstrung
plastic beads

somewhere
in the night
the last leaf falls
the sky seems
closer

THE BALCONY OF THE LORRAINE MOTEL

Memphis, Tennessee

*The Mississippi Delta begins in the lobby of the Peabody Hotel in
Memphis & ends on Catfish Row in Vicksburg.*
    — David Cohn

No, I think it begins here.
Among these rooms,
bowls of ghosts, of names.
Names that come on the breath
of thousands who have stood here.
Martin, from the Roman god of war,
the name of a saint who tore his cloak
in two to give half to a freezing beggar.
& James, brother of Jesus,
apostle, king,
assassin.

Today, this is a museum.
From the balcony where he was shot,
I look out at the period cars
staged in the parking lot.
The ones he never drove or rode in.
I look to the charred bus,
which they set on fire just a few years back
to resemble the one the Freedom Riders
took into Alabama & no further.
Here in this place of suffering,
remember the suffering.

Meanwhile, down the street,
the old tenements have twisted
into upscale apartments.
The warehouses are neon
barbecue restaurants.
The tourist couple from Parma
poses in front of the motel sign

[68]

for a selfie. Smiling. The protest woman
tells us this is not the way
he would have wanted us to remember.
These things persist
& they grow & they shift
& become what we never imagined.

The gray sky, the teal doors, the beige walls—
these are not the colors of things,
but rather the colors sent back to us.
The rejected. They are what we expect,
but in fact, they are everything but that.

So, I say this is where it begins.

Because the story you know
is not the only story. Because the blues,
the Delta, the Lorraine,
they are not simply sadnesses.
They are lights onto paths. They are ways.

BAPTIST TOWN

Greenwood, Mississippi

We drive slowly the streets of Baptist Town,
locked in by the Yazoo, the empty Union Cotton Compress,
& the tracks of the Illinois Central. With the windows
down, we smell sweet, smoky creosote seeping
from rail ties. We smell the hot water of Pelucia Bayou.
In the passenger seat she wonders why I have taken us here.
Heat mirages tremble from streets— streets
that are barely streets. Streets that have split open,
as if the old soil refused to be denied the light above.
They tell stories even in their names, the streets.
Look: there, Short crosses Young.

>   dominoes
>   on the cable-spool table—
>   mockingbirds argue

Robert Johnson lived here in 1938,
in one of the gable-roofed shotgun houses
near Walker Alley. That summer, he'd play
his blues on corners, his long fingers
pitchforking up the Stella's neck.
As the lights winked on in town,
the sheriff's curfew drove him & the others
into the jukes spotting country roads & cotton fields.
In August, he died in a Baptist Town shack, writhing,
poisoned, crawling on the ground.
If you believe the old stories.

>   from oily pavement
>   a child lifts
>   the red cowboy hat

Today, there are murals, a historical marker or two.
Folks say not to go looking for them after dark.
Nails on the porch post where someone

strung broom wire & played his blues.
A man bathes from a hose outside the firehouse,
the cool water running over his skin & pooling
among broken bottles & plastic bags
in the gutter. In the growing darkness,
light is born. Porch lights & the tiny flames
of cigarette lighters. I turn to let her know
it is time to leave.

       tiny hotel soaps
       melt in the shower setting
       closest to rain

Abbay & Leatherman Plantation

Commerce, Mississippi

> *A field of cotton—*
> *as if the moon*
> *had flowered*
>   — Matsuo Basho

In the beginning, our ancestors crawled
from a crack in the earth as locusts.
They stared at the sun as their skin hardened.
& they began to ramble.
They lost their insect bodies
& they became men & women.
& they kept rambling. They died
& were born & died & they carried
the bones of their dead everywhere
they went for centuries.
Thousands of bones.
Until the bones became more
than they were & at last,
they settled down.
They made this place a home
for their dead. They did this
before they built a home for themselves.

In 1541 de Soto crossed the Mississippi here.
Spanning the waters were the bones of his men,
his padres, our children. In 1832, Richard Abbay
bought this land from the Chickasaws.
Had his men clear & plant. Built his Big House
atop the old burial mound. Since then,
we have always known where we would be buried.
We die, we die, we die, & we are reborn every year.

By 1920, Robert Johnson lived here
with his parents. He went to school
at Indian Creek just across the road.

He learned to play mouth harp,
a little guitar. He learned to pull cotton,
haul sack. Saw men mortgage souls in scrip.
Then he left to ramble forever
as legend & returned only as legend.

In between & since these,
there were generations of ellipses.
Where the points ramble
among the spaces.
All while this land
was cut & plowed
& pared & cleared.
While children were born
in these fields,
ran in these fields,
& then they grew old & left.
Always they left—one way or another.

       your name
       the wind through the cane
       on my tongue

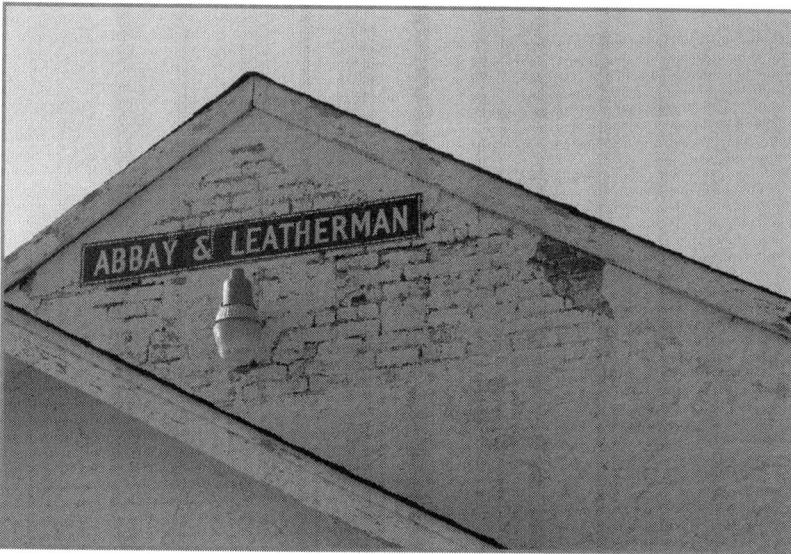

[73]

MOTHER RACHEL'S PALM & CARD

In her living room, she shows us the old book. The lists:
fantastic, nearly amusing, though we dare not let on. We sit in
high-backed chairs & read the things we never imagined could
be. Under the slow-moving ceiling fan, wrapped in a world of
green floral wallpaper.

1. Don't sweep the floor before a corpse has been
   removed from a house or you will be the next to die.
2. Never place a deathbed crossways to the world. It
   must run east to west, & the head must be toward the
   west.
3. When a man dies, cover the mirrors, stop the clocks.
4. Never wear new shoes to a funeral, or you will soon
   die.
5. ...

We read on. This grave lore. While we wait for Mother Rachel
to be ready. She has tied black ribbons on our wrists. The cat
wears a black ribbon. When Mother Rachel sits down across
from me, I mention only my dreams. Focus on her fat plastic
jewelry, almost hypnotized. Before I have finished, she tells
about the kra. An indwelling spirit that leaves the body during
death & sleep. Dreams are the adventures of the kra. Kra is the
dream-soul. Then, there is more:

6. If you go to bed thirsty at night, your dream-soul will
   wander & drink from foul puddles or fall in a well & be
   drowned.
7. A man must be awakened slowly to give his dream-soul
   time to come back. Or else he will get sick.
8. There is also the shadow soul which may be injured by
   driving a nail into one's shadow.

I stare at her milky brown eyes, nestled deep in creases. The
connection between our lives is only a few words. Dreams.
Souls. Shadows. Sleep.

9. Watch a lunar eclipse through a piece of silk to see a
   star chasing itself around the moon.

For no reason I tell her that I once tried to measure my life in eclipses. Seconds & minutes strung together over years. How old would that make me, one ring for every blackened sun, every red moon? That night, I try to stay awake to see it. I try as hard as I have tried at anything in my life.

from the moon
all earth's sunsets, dawns:
one golden ring

ARRIVING AT THE RIVERSIDE HOTEL BY NIGHT

Clarksdale, Mississippi

> *exhausted*
> *seeking an inn:*
> *wisteria flowers*
> — Matsuo Basho

In the dashboard glow, on this long stretch
through the endless cut of pines:
the children asleep in the backseat,
static-wracked blue moans on the radio:
I think about having to tell them that you had died.
I come back from some hospital, perhaps.
Crawl into bed with them as if to read a story
about rabbits or foxes.
& tell them you had died.
Whey-faced on a highway.
We pull up to the front
of the low building, its grounds sloping
abruptly down to the river bottoms,
stygian in darkness. It seems to disappear
almost as soon as it is seen.
The river & the air know no border.
We park next to an Olds Delta 88.
Its rubber, vinyl, & glass eaten
by the miasma. Metal lawn furniture
flanks the entrance, sloughing paint.
It is as if metal & brick are the only things
that can stay. We've arrived too late.
Muddy Waters lived here once. Robert Nighthawk, too.
Ike Turner, I'm told, wrote "Rocket 88"
down the hall. But before all that, in 1937,
this place was a hospital where Bessie Smith died.
They brought her here after the accident on 61 Highway.
Her half-arm pendulous,

swinging at the elbow.
She had already lost so much blood.
There was nothing that could be done.
Not in this place.
Not even for an empress.
So what chance have we?
We back the car out.
Beg the road leave our blood.

      moths in porch light
      the screen door opens
      behind me

[77]

Po' Monkey's Lounge

outside Merigold, Mississippi

Drums splash over guitar riffs.
The guitar: a sinking bell
covered in tinfoil
covered in burlap.
The bass chugging,
a barge over it. Unsteady,
I walk back. Toward the kitchen.
Four dollars over the top
of the dutch door. A woman pulls
a quart bottle of Bud
from the fridge & places it
in my hands. I ask about the tattoo
on her upper breast. She shows me
the spider behind her ear.
It's always happy hour here.
& we have hours before
we must drive home.

Christmas lights on the ceiling,
bulbs in plastic cups,
send down cones of light through smoke.
On the walls, faded beer signs.
Plastic baby dolls, impaled, naked.
The television behind the singer flickers
rhythms syncopated by the wet air.
I watch the guitarist's gold teeth flash.
From behind those sunglasses,
he could be staring at anyone.
A sinful tongue pants
within my chest. In each drop of sweat:
sin.

From somewhere, a man descends,
takes my wife's hand with pianist's fingers,
rings on most. All suit & smile.
He asks her to dance, I think,
because she grins politely,
turns to me. I nod.

At last, the pause for the cause.
She floats back to the vinyl-padded chair.
Cupping her hand over mine
on the tabletop.
I hear the soft clink of our rings.

HOOKS BROTHERS

Memphis, Tennessee

I sort pigeonholed papers.
Old manuscripts.
Never-completed to-do lists
made translucent
from being set carelessly
in oil on the kitchen counter.
Children's drawings on restaurant napkins.
Photographs.
Even the years-old junk mail
damn near makes me cry.

& then there are those scrap poems,
the ones too beautiful to finish writing,
ones that would bring us too great a sadness
if we ever thought they could really end.
There are many of those.

This was supposed to be that poem
about Hooks Brothers I promised you.
The old photography studio on Beale
we visited that drunken night
a generation after it had been converted
to a pool hall with *absinthe* in the name.

On the sidewalk, I told you how, in 1935,
Robert Johnson sat up there, dressed in pinstripes,
fedora cocked, & posed
for his only known studio portrait.
The King of the Blues on his throne atop the Delta.
I reeled off others who had been there—
Tommy Johnson, Memphis Minnie, B.B. King,
Papa Peachy Fatmouth, Jelly Roll Jerry, Blind Gin Tonic—
some I made up to see if you were sober enough

to understand. We walked in the door
as if we were one of them.
Drank whiskey all night
as if we were one of them.

At last call, you looked up
from the table & cried,
"The holes in grandmother's church fan—
the mice . . . damn, the mice . . ."

WE LET THEM THINK THEY'RE ALONE

Bayou Chene, Louisiana

Out here on the Chene, our skiffs flare out on the sides so they float high like an acorn cap. . . . This skiff floated deep and straight like a water trough or a coffin.
— Gwen Roland, *Postmark Bayou Chene*

hollow thunk of the paddle
on the hull of the canoe
the crane unfolds

its wings, angel sails,
& rises between me
& myriad cypress knees

the carpet of duckweed parts
as I set the weighted bag
into the black water

we watch it sink slowly
yet quicker than secrets
are forgotten

the bullfrogs fall silent
their bullet hole eyes
glaring upwards

as moonless night
touches foggy morning
I am still lost

A FLAME OF BEES

Brazoria County, Texas

We walk the edge of burnt broomweed
in a pasture rimmed with pin oak,
concentric circles of yellow & black.
In the old days of the Karankawa,
those best apprentices of death,
lightning fires would hold
the trees back from the prairie.
Now such things must fall
to us, we human flames,
licking black all that keeps us
from ourselves.
Today we've long forgotten
the language of air—
the way to send aloft puffs of smoke
under wet blankets,
the way to dance direction.
Each wooden frame block
is a charnel house.
Honey-meat is frozen
to crystal floes on the soil.
& everywhere the chitinous shells of bees,
piles of yellow, piles of black.
Pieces of wings float up in each footprint.
In the pond, water lilies wavering,
floats a comb, where
dozens of stingless women
who will never be mothers
still tend to eggs, beating singed wings
to cool the lost hope of children.
On the bank, nestled in clover, a soldier
waggles her figure eight,
stringing an endless knot of dust
to show the way to her bounty.

DOWN IN THE BOTTOM

on the Choctawhatchee River, Alabama

I had gone there to meet you like you asked.
Where everything seemed sprouted from the mud.
The post oak leaves, dead three autumns,
with beetles lapping each lobed curve.
The lichen-coated branches, hollowed by ants—
all the things that reminded us
that there are more than seventeen shades of brown:
not just buffed leather, burnt umber, russet,
but also horse, winter magnolia, night iris, skin.
& when I thought of you—darkness dropping
slowly down from the trees—
when I thought of you, I saw them all,
streaming warmly by like that great Muddy River.

            searching the hollows
            for our old spot
            the sphinx moth

THREE FORKS STORE

Quito, Mississippi

The night I sneaked away
from the hotel room. Left
the flowery tent of your body rising
& falling under your shallow breath.
Almost still. As if you were pretending
to be dead. I kissed the children
without waking them.
Their soft faces were ghosts
of people I did not know.
The electric blue of the bedside clock.
The deafening sound
 of hinges on the heavy door.

> the highway
> unzipped the night—
> stars fell out

Miles away, back in the trees,
behind where the store was supposed to have been.
I found an old bottle. There, by the stump
in a lace of moonlight.
Inside it were sand, rain, & a strip of burned cloth.
Long ago, the bottle was filled halfway with coal oil
& the cloth lit as a wick. Juke votives
for the midnight mass.
Gambling light. Fighting light & rubbing light.
Killing & kissing light. For the corn-cooked rounders.
The brogan-boot shufflers.
For the backdoor preachers
& their pinched choir sisters.
They lit halos in the pine straw.
But they took care there were not too many.
No one can stand too much light.

I must have thrown the bottle somewhere that night.
There, where the road forked three ways.
I must have walked back
to the car & returned to the rented bed.
I must have. But I cannot be sure.

       the bottle mouth
       when the night wind blows
       a blue voice

THE STORM AT COMMERCE LANDING

Mississippi

> *W. V. FRANCE said the school was whipped away before his eyes, as if a giant hand had snatched it up & tossed both wreckage & bodies into the boiling clouds. "Afterward men & women came to the spot," he said. "They would find a child & come crying up the road with it in their arms."*
> — Dixon (Illinois) *Evening Telegraph*, February 2, 1955

I read through the yellow paper.
How the twister hop-scotched
across the cotton fields,
landing on church,
on school, on house.
Returning the pine to dust.
Imagine that word.
Hop-scotched.
By the end,
twenty-eight schoolchildren,
teachers dead.
& also it destroyed the gin.

Today, no one remembers trees here.
& the men have become the enemies of trees
& the thought of trees. But in their place
is the wind, blowing firmly across the flat land.
Stroking the fields of cotton, fields of corn.
Mice scamper over a doll's comb
among the furrows.
Coreopsis blooms
between the floorboards.

SPOONFUL OF DIAMONDS

Dockery Farms Plantation, Mississippi

> the river below
> slow, yellow—
> the sunflower bows

The car doors slam behind us, first hers then mine.
On the river breeze, through the soaking heat,
that is how it comes. On the lithe scent of kudzu blooms,
honeysuckle, water hyacinth. The pieces
of "Spoonful Blues." A line, a lick at a time.
Over the speakers in the distant seed house rafters.
There is no one here. It is a performance of phantoms,
wind, & bees. Each footstep crunches on the shell & lime.
We follow the music back from the highway.
Past the old commissary. Past the cistern
where they baptized their children with sky.
Past the stoic gin to the weedy footprints
of the old laborer's houses. They called this *the quarters*
even then. Is it the natural way
that such beautiful places be scarred with toil?
Charley Patton came up here, of course.
The Father or Grandfather or Godfather
of the Delta Blues—I can't recall which.
Regardless, he birthed it between his wet legs,
& this is where it spilled. Every Saturday night.
Every payday. Between spells when the foremen
would run him off. He birthed his wild, frenzied sound.
Flinging, slapping his guitar. Playing behind his back.
Always growling a gravelly bass. Driving men mad
with jealousy. Ladies whipped with lust.
Either would cut him soon as buy him a drink.
& he had the smooth bronze trace
on his throat to prove it. After he was cut,
his voice changed forever. After he was cut,

[88]

the blood ran blue onto the ground.
The afterbirth of the blues.
I hold her hand as we walk the grounds,
take photos in the lazy bloom of evening.
The echoes steal into cracks of split wood.
Our footsteps sink deep into the rich mud.
We all have our origin stories.
Here: the birthplace of the blues.

      the half of her face
      in the dashboard lights
      the near side of the moon

IN GRATITUDE
Uncertain, Texas

Unseen, the cottonmouth
slips through the dirt yard
past the rusted spade.
Rivers of sand,
oxbows, bluffs
mark her path
from the bottomland
to the shade beneath
the floorboards.
There, she will lie
mouth open
eating a rain of dust
from our feet,
recalling the way
grandmother dried
snake heads
in the fireplace,
the way she ground them
to powder
& sold them as gris gris.
She will lie
white mouth open
in silent gasps
as she births
knots & knots
of requital.

SUNSET LIMITED

along the line she rides
from Pascagoula
to New Orleans

from the depot platform
where the shake & smoke
paper the sky

I listen under the rails—
carpenter ants
slowly carry the crossties away

RETURN TO AVALON

Avalon, Mississippi

in my pocket
I work the spiky sweetgum seed
a gift from my son

The black mud plumes
up behind us in the wake
of the van, like the feathers
of a massive grackle.
The man in Greenwood
had said not to stop
to ask directions on this road.
The locals think it's theirs,
& they indulge strangers
only with birdshot. In fact,
we had tried to drive it once before,
when we were years younger,
impetuous. We had turned back then,
certain the sunken cut would fold
in on us. Swallow us. Wash over us forever.

How to teach your children
about death or war or illness or age
but through cemeteries?
Even the town here is dead
& this place is its grave.
We pass through the palling dogwoods,
a natural arbor. We walk all the way back.

Mississippi John Hurt is here:
"JOHN S HURT BORN MAR 8 1892 DIED NOV 2 1968"
The quiet, humble songster,
who preferred to play house parties
& farm here in Avalon rather than ramble

through Jackson, Chicago, New Orleans.
He sang, "When my earthly trials are over,
cast my body out in the sea.
Save all the undertaker bills—
Let the mermaids flirt with me."
Cemeteries are for the living, after all,
not the dead.

        red-tailed hawk
        flushes from the grass
        beak glinting red

LOW COUNTRY ROAD

a night

so cold
we hold each
other
to keep from starving

so tired
we sleep
in the gauzy fields
of rain

so dark
our voices
themselves
are all we have

CATFISH ROW

Vicksburg, Mississippi

I got the Vicksburg blues
& I sing em anywhere I please.
That's the only thing
to give my poor heart ease.
       — Little Brother Montgomery, "Vicksburg Blues"

There is the riverboat casino,
floating, forever at berth.
We know inside,
on the ballroom dancefloor,
under massive crystal chandeliers,
there is no one. Save a man
& a woman, writing their initials
in the sweat of a morning beer.
The bottle caps under the glass bar,
each placed so precisely.
Green, red, blue, silver.
All lined up.

The fish houses, barrel houses,
sporting houses, they are all gone.
The tumbledown shacks
have fallen, too, I suppose.
Anyway, I knew them
only from songs.
We walk along the bluffs,
the dark river spreading out
on one side. The children
scour the ground,
hoping to find a yellow-gray Minié ball
left from the siege,
the kind sold in the junk shops
on Washington.

[95]

They say some still turn up
in the soil like broken worm ends
after a plowing.

We watch the children
from the shade of an ancient magnolia.
Insects gnawing the sweet centers
of the huge white blossoms.
My mother taught me
never to touch the petals.
They bruise so easily.

SOME PERSONAE

WILLIE BROWN (1900 – 1952), Delta blues guitarist & singer. Frequent accompanist to Son House & Charley Patton & early influence on Robert Johnson. Preferred to play as a side man, rather than as a soloing artist. Mentioned by name in Johnson's "Cross Road Blues." Died of heart disease before the blues revival of the 1960s.

LIZZIE DOUGLAS (1897 – 1973), aka Memphis Minnie, blues guitarist & singer. Born in Louisiana, but raised in Walls, Mississippi. Ran away to Memphis at age 13, where she performed on Beale Street. Toured with circuses & tent shows. Settled in Chicago, where she & her husband "Kansas City" Joe McCoy became part of the growing Chicago blues scene. Had an extensive recording career which spanned the 1920s – 1950s. Wrote "When the Levee Breaks" with McCoy. Langston Hughes, after seeing her perform, described her electric guitar as "a musical version of electric welders plus a rolling mill." Died in Jell Nursing Home in Memphis after her second stroke.

SON HOUSE (1902 – 1988), Delta blues guitarist & singer & sometimes preacher. Notable for his growling voice, vigorous bottleneck slide guitar technique, & confliction between a calling as a preacher & inclination toward the incompatible lifestyle of a blues performer. Played often with Charley Patton & Willie Brown in the 1930s. Served two years in the Mississippi State Penitentiary at Parchman Farm for murder in 1927. Important early influence on Robert Johnson.

JOHN HURT (1892 or '93 – 1966), blues guitarist & singer. A soft-spoken native of Avalon, Mississippi, Hurt is remembered for his quick, syncopated fingerpicking style & for the range of his repertoire. He first recorded in 1928, but after those recordings failed to sell well, he gave up on commercial recording, focusing instead on sharecropping & playing for parties, picnics, & dances around Avalon. He was located by blues enthusiast Tom Hoskins in 1963, who relied on Hurt's 1928 recording of "Avalon Blues" to guide him. Hurt reluctantly left Mississippi & became an early star of the coffeehouse & folk festival scene during the '60s blues revival.

SKIP JAMES (1902 – 1969), Delta blues guitarist, pianist, & singer. Pioneer of the so-called Bentonia sound. Noted for his dark, brooding, minor-key tunings & haunting falsetto. Recorded several songs in 1931, but became embittered with the industry after records sold poorly & his label folded, unable to pay his royalties. Rediscovered in the 1960s & performed on the blues revival circuit until his death from cancer.

ROBERT JOHNSON (1911 – 1938), described as "King of the Delta Blues." Studied under Son House, Willie Brown, & Charley Patton. Remembered for his blues virtuosity, his wide-ranging impact on blues & rock music, & his mysterious life. Associated with the Faustian legend of selling his soul to the devil in exchange for his talent. Recorded 29 songs in 1936 & '37 in Texas. Died at age 27 in Greenwood, believed to have been poisoned by a jealous husband who ran a juke joint where Johnson played.

MCKINLEY MORGANFIELD (c. 1913 – 1983), aka Muddy Waters, blues musician & father of modern Chicago blues. Born near Rolling Fork, Mississippi, he later lived on Stovall Plantation, where he worked as a tractor driver, musician, juke operator, & bootlegger. A few years after recording songs for a Library of Congress/Fisk University field unit led by Alan Lomax & John W. Work III, Waters left for Chicago where he pioneered the electric Chicago blues sound.

JELLY ROLL MORTON (1890 – 1941), New Orleans pianist & pioneer of early jazz & ragtime. Began career playing in the parlors of brothels, or "sporting houses," in New Orleans's Storyville. Remembered for his musical arrangements, & perhaps his arrogance & self-promotion, occasionally declaring himself the inventor of jazz. Toured the South in 1904, eventually making his way to Chicago, New York, & Washington, D.C.

CHARLEY PATTON (1891? – 1934), sometimes Charlie, Delta blues guitarist & singer. Widely influential, Patton revolutionized blues playing & performance, becoming one of the first great blues celebrities. His gravelly voice was emulated by many musicians, particularly Bukka White & Howlin' Wolf, & his playing style had a powerful influence on Robert Johnson & John Lee Hooker. He had a lively stage presence, playing guitar behind his back & head, beating his guitar like a drum, & stomping for percussive accompaniment. From a base on & around Dockery Farms, Patton became a top-selling superstar in his own time, playing throughout the South & as far as Chicago & New York City.

BOOKER T. WASHINGTON WHITE (1906 – 1977), aka Bukka White, Delta blues guitarist & singer. White was born in Houston, Mississippi, & as a young man, played around Clarksdale, where he first encountered Charley Patton. He had a stint as a baseball player in the Negro Leagues. Later, in 1937, he jumped bail to travel to Chicago to record. He was apprehended & sentenced to serve time at the Mississippi State Penitentiary at Parchman Farm. Upon release, he recorded a few more songs & then moved to Memphis, where he retired into obscurity. After Bob Dylan recorded his "Fixin' to Die Blues" in 1961, John Fahey & Ed Denson tracked White down in Memphis. Subsequently, he enjoyed a revived career during the '60s blues revival.

ISAIAH IKE ZIMMERMAN (1907 – 1967), sometimes Zinnerman, blues guitar player. Never recorded, but remembered for teaching Robert Johnson after Johnson left the Abbay & Leatherman Plantation near Robinsonvile. Johnson lived with Zimmerman & his family for about a year or more. The two practiced in local cemeteries to avoid being disturbed. It was when Johnson returned to the Delta after this tutelage that the legend of his selling his soul to the devil emerged. Zimmerman is suspected as the composer of several songs recorded by Johnson, including "Walking Blues" & "Come on in My Kitchen."

ACKNOWLEDGEMENTS

I offer heartfelt gratitude to the following publications in which some of these pieces first appeared, sometimes in a different version or under a different title.

AGNI—"Baptist Town"

The Arkansas Review—"Where the Southern Cross the Dog" & "Spoonful of Diamonds"

Bayou Magazine—"Beekeeping in Mississippi"

The Bitter Oleander—"Blues for Murder Only" & "Catfish Row"

Cheat River Review—"Down in the Bottom"

Chiron Review—"Three Forks Store"

Ginosko Literary Journal—"Jelly's Travels"

Illya's Honey—"Matchbox Blues"

The Louisville Review—"Return to Avalon"

Parcel—"Mother Rachel's Palm & Card"

Poets Reading the News—"When You Let Him in the Room"

Sakura Review—"Arriving at the Riverside Hotel by Night" & "Grave Decorations"

San Pedro River Review—"The World Lit by the Tail Lights of an '82 Buick"

Thanks, too, to the Poetry Society of Texas for the opportunity to publish this work, and particularly to Susan Maxwell Campbell for her direction, advice, and keen editorial talent.

"Gandy Dancing" contains lines from traditional call-&-response work songs once used by section hands while laying or maintaining railroad tracks.

"Grits Ain't Groceries" contains lines from the song "Mustang Sally" written & recorded by Mark Rice & later popularized by Wilson Pickett.

"When You Let Him in the Room" is a cento composed entirely of lines from songs recorded by Kitty Wells. These include "A Woman Never Forgets," "Do You Expect a Reward form God?," "Everybody's Somebody's Fool," "Four Walls," "Heartbreak, U.S.A.," "Heaven Says Hello," "I Can't Get There from Here," "It Wasn't God Who Made Honky Tonk Angels," "Just Beyond the Moon," "Lonely Side of Town," "Mommy for a Day," "One by One," "Open Up

Your Heart (And Let the Sunshine In)," "Queen of Honky Tonk Street," "She'll Have to Go," "She's No Angel," "That's Me without You," "The Waltz of the Angels," & "Will Your Lawyer Talk to God."

The Booker (Bukka) Washington White quote in "Wild Women Don't Have the Blues" is found in Bruce Cook's *Listen to the Blues*, New York: C. Scribner's Sons, 1973, pp. 128-129.

"Avalon" contains an excerpt from "Let the Mermaids Flirt with Me," written and recorded by "Mississippi" John S. Hurt.

All interior photographs are the work of the author, except where noted. The photograph "Poor Monkey Lounge in Merigold, Mississippi" originally appeared in *Arkansas Review*.

Cover photograph is by Wesley Tingey (www.wesleytingey.com) on Unsplash.

ABOUT THE AUTHOR

J. Todd Hawkins is a professional editor, recovering elementary teacher, and occasionally successful pee-wee soccer coach. His poetry, visual art, and literary criticism have appeared widely, including in *Arkansas Review, AGNI, Rattle: Poet's Respond, Louisville Review, Bayou Magazine, Juked, The Bitter Oleander,* and *Modern Haiku.* He is the author of the chapbooks *What Happens When We Leave* (Blackbead Press), which won the 2018 William D. Barney Memorial Chapbook Contest, as well as *Ten Counties Away* (Finishing Line Press). *This Geography of Thorns* is his first full-length poetry collection.

Hawkins is an enrolled tribal member of the Choctaw Nation of Oklahoma and a Choctaw (Chahta) Registered Literary Artist. As Chahta, he descends from ancestors who were forced from Mississippi on the Trail of Tears in the 1830s. When writing, he draws from his cultural heritage a great tradition of storytelling and a strong sense of place and attachment to the land. Passionate about the blues and bluesmakers, Hawkins has spent decades traveling widely throughout Mississippi and elsewhere in the South. He has presented at the Southern Writers/Southern Writing Conference at the University of Mississippi and has served as a panelist at the New Orleans Poetry Festival. Today, he writes and lives in Crowley, Texas, with his beloved wife and three amazing children.

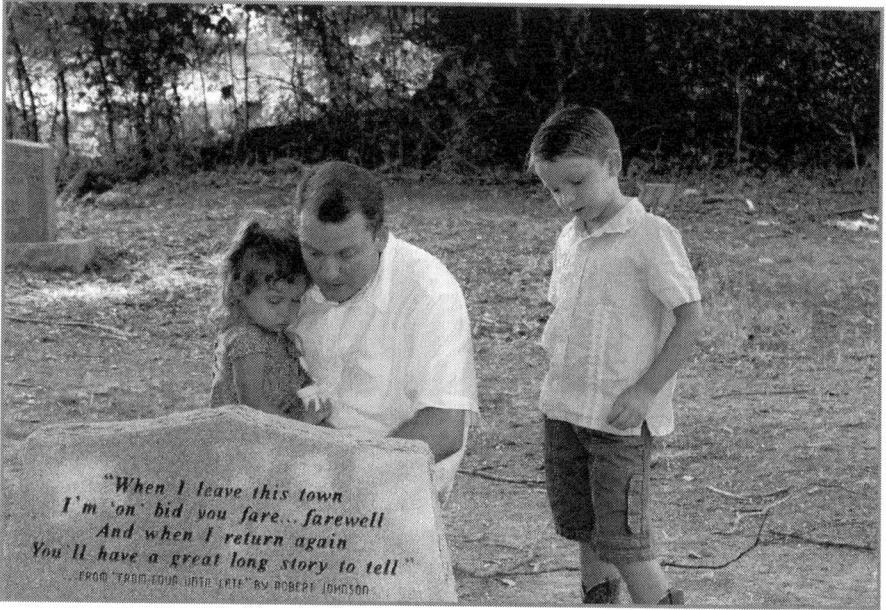

"When I leave this town
I'm 'on' bid you fare...farewell
And when I return again
You'll have a great long story to tell"
FROM "FROM FOUR UNTIL LATE" BY ROBERT JOHNSON

At the grave site of Robert Johnson, near Money, Mississippi. Pictured are the author with his son Henry & daughter Harper. Not pictured are his youngest daughter Hollis and his wife Shannon, who was serving as family photographer.

Made in the USA
Middletown, DE
04 December 2022